WORKING ANIMALS

Performers

WORKING ANIMALS

Performers

Robert Grayson

Marshall Cavendish
Benchmark
New York

This edition first published by Marshall Cavendish Benchmark in 2011
Copyright © 2011 Amber Books Ltd

Published by Marshall Cavendish Benchmark
An imprint of Marshall Cavendish Corporation

Website: www.marshallcavendish.us

This publication represents the opinions and views of the author based on Robert Grayson's personal experience, knowledge, and research. The information in this book serves as a general guide only. The author and publisher have used their best efforts in preparing this book and disclaim liability rising directly and indirectly from the use and application of this book.

Other Marshall Cavendish Offices:
Marshall Cavendish International (Asia) Private Limited, 1 New Industrial Road, Singapore 536196 • Marshall Cavendish International (Thailand) Co Ltd. 253 Asoke, 12th Flr, Sukhumvit 21 Road, Klongtoey Nua, Wattana, Bangkok 10110, Thailand • Marshall Cavendish (Malaysia) Sdn Bhd, Times Subang, Lot 46, Subang Hi-Tech Industrial Park, Batu Tiga, 40000 Shah Alam, Selangor Darul Ehsan, Malaysia

Marshall Cavendish is a trademark of Times Publishing Limited

All websites were available and accurate when this book was sent to press.

Library of Congress Cataloging-in-Publication Data

Grayson, Robert, 1951-
   Performers / Robert Grayson.
      p. cm. – (Working animals)
   Includes index.
   Summary: "Describes the role of animals in movies, sporting events, and various competitions"–Provided by publisher.
   ISBN 978-1-60870-165-0
   1. Animal training–juvenile literature. 2.
Animals–Competitions–Juvenile literature. 3. Animals on
television–Juvenile literature. 4. Animals in motion pictures–Juvenile
literature. 5. Circus animals–Juvenile literature. I. Title.

   GV1829.G73 2010
   791.3'2–dc22

                                        2010006893

Editorial and design by
Amber Books Ltd
Bradley's Close
74–77 White Lion Street
London N1 9PF
United Kingdom
www.amberbooks.co.uk

Project Editor: James Bennett
Copy Editor: Peter Mavrikis
Design: Andrew Easton
Picture Research: Terry Forshaw, Natascha Spargo

Printed in China
135642

CONTENTS

Chapter 1
Star Power

Amazing animal feats have always fascinated people. Whether it is a dog catching a Frisbee, a bear riding a bicycle, or a cat walking a tightrope, if an animal is doing something astounding, people want to see it—and always have.

As far back as ancient Rome, people went to the circus to see trained animals doing tricks. Some of those animals even got top billing. Modern-day animal performers can trace their roots back to the Middle Ages. In Europe, during the fourteenth and fifteenth centuries, people with acrobatic skills and trained animals often traveled from town to town, putting on shows for local residents. The more modern circus, with acts performed in a circular arena, debuted in 1768 in

▲ Zoe, of Friskies TV commercial fame, walks a tightrope in Boston.

◄**Buffalo Bill's Wild West Show was popular in the 1800s, especially for the astonishing feats of horsemanship that riders performed.**

❝ The first building in the United States devoted exclusively to a circus opened in 1793 in Philadelphia. ❞

London, England. This style of circus was the idea of Philip Astley, whose show featured horse-riding stunts.

Astley didn't refer to his show as a "circus," but rather as "**equestrian** arts." Charles Hughes, a business rival of Astley's, set up a similar show with all types of acts, including animal tricks, several miles away from Astley's show grounds. Hughes called his show the Royal Circus. Live animal acts soon grew in popularity and the circus quickly became established in the big city of London.

Big in the Colonies

Before the founding of the United States, during colonial times, there were always people going from one settlement to another selling their wares. Sometimes these traveling salespeople also provided the settlements with a short show featuring an animal that did tricks. The animal act attracted the children, who were soon joined by their parents.

The first building in the United States devoted exclusively to a circus opened in 1793 in Philadelphia. Known as the Circus of Pépin and Breschard, it included a number of animal acts. George Washington was among the dignitaries who attended one of the shows.

◄ **Wonder horse Marocco dazzled audiences in the 1500s by standing on his hind legs.**

In the nineteenth century, several large circuses toured the United States with live animal performers, but those circuses mostly traveled to big cities. In the rough-and-tumble West, where territories were still being settled, small acts, called dog-and-pony shows, provided the pioneers with entertainment.

In the 1800s, there were no schools where people could learn how to train animals to do tricks. Training animals was a skill that was handed down from generation to

▲ In the 1800s, dog-and-pony acts like this one delighted both youngsters and adults.

"Sometimes vaudeville acts combined talents. A comedian might tell jokes while his dog performed tricks."

generation. Most people learned how to work with animals onstage by watching others do it or by serving as an apprentice to an animal trainer.

Buffalo Bill's Wild West

One of the most famous circuslike touring shows in the nation was started in 1883 by William "Buffalo Bill" Cody. Called Buffalo Bill's Wild West Show, it included a variety of animal acts, especially horse-riding stunts and tricks.

Animal acts were common in the heyday of vaudeville. Vaudeville shows—a form of theatrical entertainment that was popular from the 1880s through the early 1930s—put together a variety of unrelated live performances on the same bill. These performances ranged from dancers and singers to comedians and animal acts. Sometimes the acts combined talents. A comedian might tell jokes while his dog performed

tricks. These shows traveled throughout the United States and Canada, and some became quite well known.

On the Silver Screen

When silent movies first hit the big screen in the 1890s, it did not take long for filmmakers to introduce horses into this new form of entertainment. After all, a director couldn't make a Western without

▼ **In the 1930s, a crowd gathers to watch an unusual animal act, an elephant riding a tricycle.**

What a Zoo!

One of the great moviemakers of the silent film era was Mack Sennett. Numerous actors and comics worked for Mack Sennett. He also employed a number of animal actors, from Teddy the Wonder Dog (a Great Dane) and Teddy's close friend and co-star, Pepper (a cat), to Wilhelm (a white mouse), Anna May (an elephant), and Numa and Duke (lions). Most of the time, these animals played comedy roles, appearing regularly in Sennett films, including the famous Keystone Cops movies.

▲ **On the set of a Mack Sennett film, actors and their canine co-star take a break.**

"Moviemakers wondered if other animals could take to the screen, play big roles, and perhaps even become movie stars themselves."

horses! With horses regularly appearing in film, moviemakers wondered if other animals could take to the screen, play big roles, and perhaps even become movie stars themselves.

In 1912, a young writer brought a script to the head of a movie studio called New York Vitagraph. The script called for a dog to play a daring role, saving the film's hero. The studio paid the writer ten dollars for the script

▼ **Actress Eleanor Boardman rides a trained Bactrian camel in the 1932 silent movie *Souls for Sale.***

"When Jean's owner gave the command, the dog untied the actor in seconds, and the canine world got its first leading lady—Jean the Vitagraph Dog."

and the search was on to cast the **canine** star.

The dog's part in the movie was complicated because it required the canine hero to do a wide range of tricks. Though many dogs were tested for the part, none could handle the demands of the role until one day Vitagraph's biggest star, Florence Turner, saw a collie playing with her owner outside the studio. The actress, who liked the collie's looks and was impressed by the tricks she could do, approached the pair and invited them to meet the head of the studio.

Vitagraph's co-founder, Albert E. Smith, told the collie's owner that if the dog, named Jean, could untie the human hero's hands and feet, she would have the part in the movie. When Jean's owner gave the command, the dog untied the actor in seconds, and the canine world got its first leading lady— Jean the Vitagraph Dog. As soon as Jean appeared on-screen, she was a hit, and moviegoers wanted more.

◀ **Jean the Vitagraph Dog paved the way for later canine film stars.**

A Great Pal

When dog trainer Rudd Weatherwax first met Pal in the early 1940s, the male collie was uncontrollable and simply refused to behave. His owner, who had almost given up on him, approached Weatherwax in hopes that the trainer could tame the disobedient dog. He did, but when Weatherwax called the man to pick up the dog, Pal's owner said he did not want him anymore and asked if Weatherwax would keep him. The trainer agreed.

Weatherwax taught Pal to do a lot of tricks, and in 1943 he brought the canine

to a film studio to audition for a role as a stunt dog in the movie *Lassie Come Home*. Pal got the job as the double for the dog playing Lassie. Early in the filming, a scene called for Lassie to jump into a raging river and make a rescue. The collie playing Lassie refused to go into the river, so Pal was brought in. Not only did Pal jump into the water, swim against the current, and make the rescue, but he came out of the water, shook himself off, and collapsed for the cameras like a true star. The movie's director, Fred Wilcox, proclaimed that "Pal might have jumped into the water, but Lassie came out." As a result of that performance, Pal was given the lead role in the movie and gained worldwide fame as Lassie in five additional films.

▲ **Lassie was one of the most popular actors—canine or otherwise—Hollywood ever produced.**

Costume Classic

In 1995 the Public Broadcasting Service (PBS) decided to try to get children interested in literary classics by introducing the books through a dog with an incredible imagination. The television show featured a dog that would daydream about being the lead character in classic adventures like Robin Hood, Sherlock Holmes, or Oliver Twist. He would even envision himself dressed in period costumes from the story! The shows also featured the dog's young owner, Joe, and his friends. All of the stories were narrated by the dog himself, in the voice of actor Larry Brantley. The stories were told just as they were written by their original authors.

▲ **Wishbone wears one of his famous period costumes.**

The canine character, named Wishbone, was played by Soccer, a Jack Russell terrier that showed his emotions and had body language much like that of a human actor. The show's producers auditioned one hundred dogs before casting Soccer in the lead role. Soccer did not mind the many costume changes or the rigorous filming schedule required by the Emmy Award–winning show.

Wishbone, which ran from 1995 to 1998, is still in reruns and can be seen on DVD as well. Soccer even played Wishbone in a made-for-TV movie called *Wishbone's Dog Days of the West*. Books were released in conjunction with the television series. All of the book covers featured Soccer in full period costume!

Chapter 2
Now That's Entertainment!

Soon after Jean the Vitagraph Dog became famous, moviemakers realized how popular animals could be as entertainers. So it didn't take them long before they began casting all kinds of animals in their films.

But it took more than just the ability to do tricks for animals to star in movies. They had to have talent, and they had to be well trained.

On stage, animals usually worked directly with their trainers. The two rehearsed together and often performed together. For movies, the animals rehearsed their tricks with their trainers over and over again, but when it came time to perform the tricks before the camera, it was with an actor, not the trainer. The trainer would stand offscreen and shout out

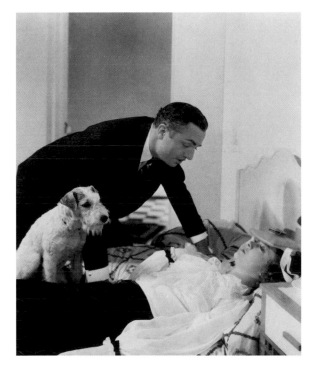

◄ *Wizard of Oz* legend Toto appears with Judy Garland in 1939.

▲ William Powell and Asta tend to Myrna Loy in *The Thin Man* in 1934.

And the Winner Is...

In 1951, the American Humane Association started giving out awards for outstanding animal performances in movies. Known as the Patsy Awards, they were considered the Oscars for animals. Soon, animal performances in television, commercials, and onstage were also recognized by the awards. Many animal actors were honored until the program was discontinued in 1986.

▲ **Cheetah appears with his acting buddy Lex Barker, better known as Tarzan.**

commands. The animal, who would have to perform the trick with a different person, could not afford to be unnerved by the change. Sometimes actors just didn't relate well to animals. For animal actors to be successful, they had to give a great performance even if their human co-star had a fussy temperament.

Animals also had to cope with the technical aspects of this new medium. For instance, they could not be scared by the bright lights used to film scenes. Some animals became frightened when the harsh lights were turned on just as filming was about to begin. Other animals were uncomfortable by the heat the lights gave off. But those animals who made it in the film business shrugged off these small irritations, proving to be true professionals.

Brownie's Big Break

Not all animals succeeded as actors, but some were naturally talented. Brownie, a small, homeless dog, was wandering the streets of California one day, sniffing around for some food in an alley, when a

"*Animals also had to cope with the technical aspects of this new medium. For instance, they could not be scared by the bright lights used to film scenes.*"

dogcatcher spotted him. The dogcatcher tried to capture Brownie, but the pooch put up quite a fight. Charles Gee, a passerby, came to the dog's rescue.

After the scuffle died down, Gee gave the dogcatcher a few dollars for his trouble and said he would take the dog home. As Gee and his newly adopted dog got acquainted, he noticed that the dog could perform tricks effortlessly.

Gee didn't think much about it until a friend mentioned that Charlie Chaplin, the famous film star, was looking for a dog to play opposite

▼ **Canine star Brownie with Charlie Chaplin and Edna Purviance in *A Dog's Life*.**

" When people saw the hero dog on-screen, they quickly fell in love with him…. Rin Tin Tin went on to make twenty-five more movies for the studio… and helped build Warner Bros. into a motion picture giant. "

him in *A Dog's Life*. Chaplin called in dozens of dogs for a **screen test** but none were right for the part until Brownie took center stage.

When Brownie tried out for the part, he worked perfectly with Chaplin. The two instantly bonded and the movie became a classic. Brownie, a natural on the screen without a trace of training, went on to make many more movies and never went hungry again.

A Hero Dog

By the time Rin Tin Tin debuted in his first movie in 1922, a little-known studio called Warner Bros. was on the verge of bankruptcy. When people saw the hero dog on-screen, they quickly fell in love with him. A German

▶ **Rin Tin Tin howls to get help for a fallen comrade.**

A Canine Author

Dogs have appeared on television and on the Broadway stage, in movies and commercials, and one has even written his own autobiography. Moose, the Jack Russell terrier that played Eddie for eleven seasons on the Emmy Award-winning show *Frasier*, published his life story in 2000 with the help of human writer Brian Hargrove. The book, titled *My Life as a Dog*, tells the tale of Moose's rise to fame in the dog's own words. It begins with his days as a hard-to-control pet and traces his life through his first television commercial for the Louisiana State Lottery to his audition for the sitcom *Frasier* and his days on the set.

Moose recalls his first flight from the East Coast to Los Angeles, which he made in a crate, noting that he could not help but think that "Tom Cruise doesn't travel like baggage."

In the book, Moose expresses his feelings toward his trainer and the actors he works with on *Frasier*, and writes that he should have won an Emmy for his work in the pilot episode of the show.

When the book came out, *Frasier* was only in its sixth season out of an eventual eleven. But Moose never wrote a second book, even though his first book sold very well. *My Life as a Dog* also included pictures from the Moose family album.

▲ **Moose with his *Frasier* co-stars. The show ran from 1993 to 2004.**

"When silent movies gave way to 'talkies' in 1927, animals moved into the new era as well."

Shepherd, Rin Tin Tin went on to make twenty-five more movies for the studio, working up until his death in 1932, and helped build Warner Bros. into a motion picture giant.

When silent movies gave way to "talkies" in 1927, animals moved into the new era as well. Though some people thought that animal sounds would be unpleasant to hear, audiences disagreed. They loved hearing animals bark, meow, moo, and whinny. In fact, one animal even talked. In 1950, Universal Studios put

◄ **German shepherds follow commands from their trainer, Moe Di Sesso, as the cameras roll.**

▲ **Actor Donald O'Connor listens intently to Francis the Talking Mule in one of the seven comedies the mule made.**

"*During the 1950s, many animals starred in their own television shows. Lassie and Rin Tin Tin went from the big screen to the small screen.*"

out the comedy movie *Francis*, the story of an army mule that befriends a young soldier named Peter Stirling and gives him great insight into solving military problems. Francis can talk, but chooses to speak only to Peter—and only when they are alone. When Francis is on-screen, the mule's mouth moves as if the animal were actually talking. The film was so successful that the studio made six additional movies.

Star Turns

Movies turned many animals into film stars. Some of the popular animal characters on film include Lassie, Benji, Air Bud, Underdog, Roy Rogers's horse Trigger and his dog Bullet, as well as Toto—Dorothy's black terrier in *The Wizard of Oz*—and Cheetah, the chimpanzee in the Tarzan movies.

Talking movies presented new challenges to animal actors. Now not only did trainers have to stay off camera, they could no longer shout out commands because the movie sound track could pick up their voices. So animal actors had to be taught to work on cue by following hand signals trainers gave them from behind the cameras. Animals that could not learn hand signals had little chance of making it in talking movies.

During the 1950s, many animals starred in their own television shows. Lassie and Rin Tin Tin went from the big screen to the small screen. Others soon followed, creating popular television shows including *Gentle Ben, Flipper,* and *Mr. Ed*—a talking horse similar to Francis the mule.

Animals played a major role in television commercials as well, with

▶ **Several cats have played Morris, the advertising mascot for 9Lives brand cat food, since the 1960s.**

Panther

Panther, a talented orange tabby cat, was found in a shelter by animal trainer Bill Casey, who nursed him back to health. It took nearly a year for the very affectionate but thin cat to get well again. Panther did a few television commercials, but never landed a big part until he was cast in a television show called *Early Edition*. The show was about a man who gets tomorrow's news today by receiving a newspaper with the next day's headlines a day early. The man, played by Kyle Chandler, then tries to stop disasters before they happen.

The newspaper was delivered daily by a cat that seemingly came out of nowhere, played by Panther. The cat's meow signaled the paper's arrival each day. Panther was eight years old when he filmed the first show and was nine in 1996 when CBS decided to air the series. Following the first season, Panther came down with a serious illness that required lifesaving surgery. The cat had the procedure and recovered to return for the rest of the show's run through 2000. After he came back from sick leave, Panther had an understudy named Carl, but did most of the acting in the show himself. When *Early Edition* went off the air, Panther, considered a senior animal actor by then, retired to a life of leisure.

▶ **Lead actors Panther and Kyle Chandler frolic on the set of the TV show *Early Edition*.**

a finicky **feline** named Morris becoming a popular "spokes cat" for a line of cat food products.

Animals also left big pawprints on Broadway productions, including Sandy, a mixed-breed dog in the show *Annie* from 1977 to 1983, and a Chihuahua who played Bruiser in *Legally Blonde: The Musical* from 2007 to 2008.

Safeguarding Animal Rights

In 1940, the American Humane Association (AHA) established a film and television unit to safeguard the rights of animals being used on both the big and small screen. The association is the only organization that has **jurisdiction** on a movie set to make sure no animals are harmed in the making of movies and television shows. AHA representatives travel to filming locations throughout the United States and around the world, protecting the rights of animal actors and making sure that no one is abusing them.

▶ **Reese Witherspoon carries canine lead Bruiser in a scene from *Legally Blonde.***

Chapter 3
Working in Sports

They have names like Join in the Dance, Mine That Bird, Musket Man, and Dunkirk, and they are all elite animal athletes in one of the world's most popular sports: horse racing.

Horse racing dates back more than 4,500 years, when horses were first **domesticated**. The sport of horses carrying riders and racing against one another was part of the ancient Greek Olympics more than 2,500 years ago.

In twelfth-century England, knights riding on horseback raced before a crowd of onlookers. By the early 1700s, racetracks were found all across England, and races featured a number of horses, with fans often betting on which one would win.

◀ **Jockey Edgar Prado crosses the finish line riding Barbaro to win the 132nd Kentucky Derby in 2006.**

▲ **Riders compete in the Belmont Stakes, a horse race that began in the 1860s.**

▲ Lightweight and agile, jockeys wear brightly colored outfits for identification during a horse race.

« The sport of horses carrying riders and racing against one another was part of the ancient Greek Olympics. »

Big Business

The first racetrack on American shores was built on Long Island in the mid-1600s. Horse racing was a local sport in America for many years, usually as the highlight of a regional fair. In the late 1860s, it became organized as a national sport. Today the most popular form of horse racing is **thoroughbred** racing, a sport that has produced star horses like Man o' War, Seabiscuit, Seattle Slew, and Secretariat. Horses with riders compete against one

▼ **Seabiscuit arrives at Santa Anita Park in Arcadia, California, in 1938. His trainer, Tom Smith, leads him while his owner, C. S. Howard, walks alongside.**

"*Owning a racehorse is considered a business venture. Because it is very expensive to buy and keep racehorses, they are usually owned by a group of investors.*"

another around a dirt track five to twelve furlongs long. (A furlong is one-eighth of a mile, or 660 feet.)

Owning a racehorse is considered a business venture. Because it is very expensive to buy and keep racehorses, they are usually owned by a group of investors. Over the course of their careers, successful racehorses can earn a great deal of money for their owners. One of horse racing's biggest events is the Kentucky Derby, held in Louisville, Kentucky, every May.

Harnessing Fans' Enthusiasm

Harness racing, another form of competition for horse and rider, goes back to ancient Roman chariot races. Harness racing is popular in many countries today, including the United States, Canada, New Zealand, Australia, the United Kingdom, France, and Italy. In the United

▲ **Most harness races cover a distance of one mile (1.6 kilometers).**

▶ **A horse and driver hit top speed during a harness race in Ohio.**

"Each harness race features a number of horses and drivers competing against one another. A day at the harness races usually includes ten races."

States, harness racing started in the late 1700s, when it was a common rural pastime. People in two-wheeled carts, pulled by horses, raced against one another on dirt roads.

Harness racing tracks were first constructed in the United States in the early 1800s. Many of the tracks were built at fairgrounds, where the sport rapidly became a big attraction. By this time, harness racing had evolved into the sport it is today, where a horse pulls a professional driver in a two-wheeled cart, called a **sulkie**. Each race features a number of horses and drivers competing against one another. A day at the harness races usually includes ten races.

Steeplechase

In the sport of steeplechase, highly trained and well-**conditioned** horses with riders navigate a course of obstacles, such as stone walls and water jumps. The horses competing in these events must have great timing and be tireless jumpers. Strong legs are especially important for these equine athletes.

◀ **Obstacles in steeplechase racing are sometimes collapsible, so as not to injure the horses.**

▲ A horse and rider make a dramatic jump.

« Polo ponies need to have great stamina and strength. They have to be able to maneuver quickly, and take the hits when they bump into other speeding horses. »

In the 1700s, during the early days of the sport, it was natural obstacles found along cross-country trails that stood in the horses' way. The death-defying dangers included ditches, fences, ponds, and high brush. Today human-made obstacles make up a course that at times is no less dangerous than the natural ones. Steeplechase competitions are held in the United Kingdom, Ireland, France, Australia, Canada, and the United States. They are also part of the Summer Olympics.

Hardly "Ponies"

For polo, a team sport played on horseback, horses have to be fast and **agile**. While they are called "polo ponies," they are actually fully grown horses, weighing more than 1,000 pounds (450 kilograms). Each horse carries a rider, who uses a **mallet** to hit a ball into the opponents' goal. The field of play is 300 yards (275 meters) long and there are usually four mounted players on each team. A game can last between four and eight periods of seven minutes each.

Polo ponies need to have great stamina and strength. They have to be able to maneuver quickly, and take the hits when they bump into other speeding horses. Horses used in polo must be able to respond under pressure with sudden bursts of speed, yet stay calm. A polo pony can't lose its temper.

Well-Treated or Mistreated?

Though horse racing in all its forms has many fans, some people charge that sports involving horses amount to a form of animal abuse.

▶ **It takes a powerful horse to compete in a polo match. A polo player and his pony practice for hours to develop a winning form.**

Dancing Horses

The internationally famous and highly skilled Lipizzaner stallions perform amazing ballet moves to music. They are considered the world's only true dancing horses.

The specially bred white horses begin their training when they are four years old and the learning process takes roughly six years to complete. When a young horse begins training, it is always matched with an experienced rider who patiently teaches the horse all the complicated moves in stages. Many of the moves are performed in midair, with the horse having all four feet off the ground!

These horses were first bred in the sixteenth century in Spain for use by the military and Spanish nobility. The horses were as agile in war as they are while dancing. The muscular, hardworking, athletic Lipizzaner has a deep chest with strong legs. These animals are very intelligent but mature slowly. The stallions are able to continue to perform into their twenties and many of the horses live for thirty years or more.

Lipizzaner horses have showcased their skills throughout the world and have entertained millions over the years, including heads of state. These talented animals have been featured in many television shows and movies and are the subject of countless books as well as newspaper and magazine articles. Lipizzaner is a rare breed with only about three thousand known to exist.

▲ **This Lipizzaner stallion performs dazzling dance moves during a show at the HP Pavilion in San José, California.**

Opponents claim, for example, that racehorses are not treated humanely because they are forced to race before they are old enough to race safely, which results in injuries.

Yet owners of horses in sports counter that these animals are valuable, exceptional athletes, and are treated accordingly. They are given the best food, prime living quarters, and top medical attention. A team of experts works with the horses, making sure, the owners say, that every precaution is taken to safeguard the health and welfare of each of these equine athletes.

▲ **With a jockey pushing hard, this horse speeds toward the finish line, leaving all challengers in the dust.**

Chapter 4
Animal Competitions

Throughout the world, there are a variety of shows and competitive events for all sizes and types of animals. The animals competing in these events are highly trained athletes and respond by giving nothing less than their very best.

Top Dogs

Most of the events that trained and athletic dogs participate in have separate governing bodies that establish rules and qualifications for contestants. Dogs can compete in local and international agility competitions, in which they go in turn through an obstacle course that includes tunnels, jumps, hurdles, and **weave poles.** The winner of this timed event is the dog that gets through the course the fastest without committing any faults.

◄ **A Shih Tzu jumps a hurdle at a World Series dog show in Texas.**

▲ **An energetic and well-trained dog catches a Frisbee.**

Bunny Hop

For several decades rabbits have been showing off their athletic abilities in jumping and agility competitions, and these sports are beginning to find an audience worldwide. Rabbit-jumping competitions started in Sweden in the late 1970s and gained international attention when they were shown on British television in the 1980s.

Once the jumping competitions caught on, rabbit agility contests began to take hold as well, many in the United States at state fairs and 4-H youth club events. In rabbit jumping, bunnies leap over fences of various heights to see which can jump the highest. Besides Sweden, rabbit jumping is popular in Denmark and Finland. There are more than fifty rabbit-jumping clubs in those three countries alone, and clubs are beginning to appear in England and the United States, too.

Rabbit agility is much like dog agility, with competitors maneuvering around an obstacle course in a timed event to see which one can make it through the fastest.

Dogs that compete in the Frisbee competition showcase their skills at catching and retrieving a flying disk, usually thrown by their owner. Events include short- and long-distance throws. This competition is a team sport, and both humans and canines must know each other's moves very well. This sport takes meticulous coordination.

Weight pulling is a test of strength, with dogs pulling objects on snow using sleds and on land using carts. There are different classes of competition, based on the size and weight of the dog.

Dogs that love the water and like to swim usually turn out to be great at dock jumping. This sport tests how far a dog can jump from a dock into the water. The dog works with a trainer but does the jump alone. The dock is usually 40 feet (12 meters) long and covered with turf so the dog can get a good running start. The water has to be at least 4 feet (1.2 meters) deep. This event has

▶ **A well-trained dog excels during a weight-pulling competition in Minsk, Belarus.**

❝Humans and dogs with a good sense of timing can show off during freestyle obedience competitions.❞

become very popular at fairs around the world.

Humans and dogs with a good sense of timing can show off during freestyle obedience competitions when **synchronized** moves make the difference between winners and runners-up. Set to music, this sport shows just how well trained a dog is, as it is led through jumps, weaves, and various other motions by its trainer.

Flyball is a dog relay team sport. Teams of four dogs run a course of hurdles to get to a spring-loaded box that releases a tennis ball. Each dog runs one leg of the race and the last member of the team hits the box that

▲ **A black Labrador retriever completes a jump during a dock-diving competition. Dogs that excel in this sport love being in the water.**

Sporting Camels

In some parts of the world, especially the Middle East, camel racing is a major sport. Camel racing started in ancient times when nomadic people would race their camels against each other for fun. Today smaller camels are bred to be racers. The camels begin training when they are six months old but do not start to compete until they are three years old. Camels can run up to 40 miles (64 kilometers) an hour.

In camel racing each camel carries a jockey and, as in horse racing, the jockeys are usually short and thin. They must display great balance to stay on the camel. Races last about ten to fifteen minutes and span 3 to 6 miles (5–10 kilometers). In parts of the Middle East, camel racing is big business, with camel-racing tracks becoming major tourist attractions. People in other countries have taken note of camel racing's growing popularity and are picking up on this new sport. Australia hosts the annual Camel Cup races and several other major races in the sport as well.

▲ **Camel racing is a major sport in the United Arab Emirates. Young Pakistani boys are serving as jockeys in this race in Dubai.**

"Sheepdog trials are based on obedience and speed. As with many other competitions, human and canine must be able to work extremely well together."

releases a ball into the air. The dog catches the ball, and then runs the ball back to the finish line. Each dog has to learn its role and do it well for a team to win at flyball consistently.

Sheepdog trials are very popular contests used to determine the best sheepherding dog in the competition. Border collies usually excel in this sport, but other breeds participate as well. Some competitions only allow herding breeds to enter these contests, while other trials permit any dog trained to herd to enter. The hit movie *Babe* was about a pig that was trained by Border collies and was entered into a sheepherding contest.

The sport's first contest is traced back to Bala, Wales, in 1873 and has been a mainstay at agricultural fairs ever since. Sheepdog trials are based on obedience and speed. As with many other competitions, human and canine must be able to work extremely well together. Australia also holds cattle-dog trials for dogs that excel at herding cattle.

Agile Cats

Cat agility competitions, held at major cat shows, are slowly growing

▲ **A Rottweiler participates in a heated flyball competition.**

▶ **A shepherd and her Border collie compete in a sheepdog trial in Scotland.**

Monkey Business

Whiplash is a capuchin monkey that dresses up in a cowboy outfit and rides a Border collie at rodeos throughout Europe and North America. He has been on sports programs and other network television shows, has made a series of television commercials for a fast-food chain, and travels the world, showing off his balancing act. He has performed for more than twenty years, starting when he was just two years old.

▲ **A multicolored tabby walks along a fence during a cat agility competition.**

▲ **Whiplash shows off his skill at a rodeo.**

in popularity. Like participants in the dog competitions, these cats must make their way through an obstacle course, showing their speed, intelligence, coordination, and ability to follow their owner's commands. It takes a special kind of cat to excel in these events but, if trained as kittens, talented felines can claw their way to the top of the sport.

On a Roll

Another amazing animal sport is pigeon tumbling or pigeon rolling. This sport is popular all over the world. With the right diet, exercise, and training, birds born with the talent to

« Pigeons also race, leaving from a predetermined location miles from their lofts. The birds are timed on how long it takes them to return home. »

flip backwards can become champion rollers. Pigeons trained in this sport can flip backwards and then continue to rotate as they make a spinning descent that seems as though they are falling lifelessly out of the sky. Then they pull out of the dive and shoot back up into the sky. Some pigeons can practically touch the ground before they start to fly upward again.

In many competitions the bird must dive below 2 feet (61 centimeters) from the ground and fly back up at least 10 feet (3 meters) for its dive to count for points. Pigeons also race, leaving from a predetermined location miles from their **lofts**. The birds are timed on how long it takes them to return home.

▲ **A man gets things going at the starting line of a pigeon-rolling competition in Jacksonville, Florida.**

Chapter 5
Career Guide

The field of animal training covers a wide range of jobs and offers a number of opportunities for people interested in working with animals.

Many local pet shops have people working right in the store who know how to train animals in the basics, such as obedience. Some trainers work in marine parks, such as Sea World, or at zoos, training animals and putting on shows with them. Circuses employ animal trainers as well, and many professionals train animals for parts in movies, on television, and on stage.

Among the key requirements for training animals are a love and respect for these creatures. Before

◄ **A trainer works with dolphins during a show in Tenerife, Spain.**

▲ **Horses listen intently to their trainer at a French circus.**

" Training animals is a learning process for the trainers and each of the animals. A challenging job, training animals can also be very satisfying and rewarding. "

pursuing a career in this field, people should also know what kind of animals they enjoy working with. Some people can train all kinds of animals, but others prefer big animals, small animals, reptiles, just

dogs, or just cats. Trainers do a better job working with animals they can relate to, and that works well for the animals, too.

Talent Scouts

Trainers must be able spot the potential talent in each animal they work with. This takes both time and patience, as well as knowing how to teach and reward animals. Trainers must be firm yet compassionate when correcting animals that make mistakes. Training animals is a learning process for the trainers and each of the animals. A challenging job, training animals can also be very satisfying and rewarding.

Many zoos, marine parks, aquariums, racetracks, and even animal talent agencies look for people who want to be animal

▲ **A young girl learns to train a horse to perform circus tricks.**

▶ **Training your pet can be an enjoyable and rewarding task.**

A Hollywood Inn

Frank Inn was one of the most famous animal trainers in Hollywood. He trained animals for movies and television for more than fifty years and worked with dogs, cats, pigs, and chimps, to name just a few. His cat Orangey made many movies, including the 1961 hit *Breakfast at Tiffany's*, starring Audrey Hepburn. His dog Higgins was famous as the first dog to play the lead in the *Benji* series. Besides being Benji, Higgins played Dog in the TV series *Petticoat Junction*.

▶ **Frank Inn shares a light moment with Higgins.**

trainers and will teach them the skills they need to be successful at it. These animal habitats, attractions, and companies are looking for individuals who have some background in animal studies. Zoos and marine parks are especially interested in people with college degrees in biology, zoology, or animal psychology. Though a college degree is not absolutely necessary to break into the field, it does give someone an advantage over a person who has no background in animal studies at all. Even taking just a few college-level courses in animal studies would give a candidate for an animal trainer's position an edge.

▶ **Sea lions are always ready to play ball, and their trainers know it. Here they prepare for a show for vacationers.**

Experience Wanted

Experience working with animals will also help someone break into the animal-training field. Candidates for animal training are advised to do some volunteer work at a zoo, in a veterinarian's office, or at a stable. The more experience people have working with all kinds of animals, the better their chances of breaking into the field of animal training.

Even today, most people learn how to train animals by apprenticeship, watching and working with someone who has lifelong experience training animals. Some experienced animal trainers teach courses in training animals, and some colleges—but not many—are beginning to offer courses or programs in training animals as well.

Zoos, marine parks, aquariums, and circuses like to hire their animal

▶ **Hollywood director David R. Ellis cues a canine actor.**

Get the Movie Bug

People who study insects can find work in Hollywood. Some film scripts call for on-screen insects and somebody has to train them. Entomologists—people who study insects—work part-time as trainers for insects set to star, or at least appear, in movies or television shows.

Insects cannot be trained like dogs and cats, so entomologists have to make sure that the set for a film featuring insects is built in a way that prompts the bugs to do what the script calls for. For instance, insects might be lured in a particular direction on the set because a food the bugs like draws them toward it. The food has to be positioned in exactly the right place—not too high, not too low. If insects are supposed to go to a certain place on the set and are attracted by lights, the lights have to be set up right where the bugs are supposed to end up. It is also the job of the entomologists to make sure the sets are constructed so the insects will not be harmed in any way. Insects appear in horror or adventure films more than any other types of films.

Big Game

Not all animal actors are dogs or cats. Many movie and television scripts call for tigers, lions, elephants, bears, and other exotic animals, and it takes an extraordinary kind of trainer to work with those animals. Some trainers specialize in working with big cats, bears, monkeys, or other wild animals. These trainers have often worked with these animals for years, because it is best to start training exotic animals from the time they are born. Many of these animals simply cannot be trained if the process starts too late in life.

It is important for the trainer to know the animal well and know how the animal will react in every situation. The trainer has to know what time of day is best to work with the animal, when to take breaks to feed the animal, and when the animal is beginning to get tired and needs to sleep.

▲ **Training big game is highly specialized work.**

Trainers of exotic animals usually work in large compounds where the animals can wander freely and be trained in an atmosphere as close to their natural habitat as possible. However, even a well-trained animal can misbehave and turn on its trainer, so there is always an element of danger when working with animals that normally live in the wild. People who have the patience and talent to train exotic animals are highly sought after in the entertainment world.

trainers from within the organization. Finding a job—or apprenticeship—working with animals in these places gives a person an inside track on getting considered for an animal training job. These organizations like to see how a person relates to and cares for the animals. They want to make sure an employee has the right temperament to be an animal trainer and is serious about the work. Once selected, a great deal of time and effort will be devoted to teaching the new employee how to be an excellent animal trainer so that skills can eventually be passed on to someone else.

Safety a Top Priority

The field of animal training has changed a great deal from the days of the dog-and-pony shows. Animal safety is a top priority. Much more is being done to ensure that animals are properly cared for, get appropriate medical attention, are transported safely, and have suitable housing facilities. Animal trainers must be aware of the latest concerns and laws to protect animal performers.

▲ **An animal trainer knows how to take good care of his charge.**

Glossary

agile
able to move smoothly, easily, and quickly

canine
relating to dogs

conditioned
made accustomed to or used to something

domesticated
tamed for use by humans

equestrian
relating to horses

feline
relating to cats

jurisdiction
authority over a particular group

lofts
buildings used to house pigeons

mallet
a hammerlike object with a long stick used in the sport of polo

screen test
a short film, used as a test, to see how an actor (even an animal actor) looks on-screen

sulkie
a two-wheeled cart drawn by a horse in harness racing

synchronized
perfectly coordinated, as in a dance move

thoroughbred
a purebred, most commonly used to refer to a racehorse bred to run fast

weave poles
a line of poles past which a dog must run, alternately passing to the left and right of each pole

Further Information

BOOKS

Carroll, Willard. *I, Toto: The Autobiography of Terry, the Dog Who Was Toto.* New York: Stewart, Tabori & Chang, 2001.

Helfer, Ralph. Zamba: *The True Story of the Greatest Lion That Ever Lived.* New York: HarperCollins , 2005.

Moose, with Brian Hargrove. *My Life as a Dog.* New York: HarperEntertainment Books, 2000.

Silverman, Stephen. *Movie Mutts: Hollywood Goes to the Dogs.* New York: Harry N. Abrams, 2001.

WEBSITES

www.lassie.com
Official site of the world's most famous dog.

www.seaworld.org/animal-info/info-books/training/animal-training-careers.htm
Contains valuable information on how to train for jobs working with animals.

www.whiplashrides.com
Official site of Whiplash the monkey.

www.theatricalanimals.com
Includes interesting information about training and working with animals on Broadway.

http://horsefame.tripod.com/
Contains information about horses in movies and on television.

Index

PICTURE CREDITS

The photographs in this book are used by permission and through the courtesy of:

Alamy: 9 (Vintage Images), 33 (Stan Rohrer), 47 (David Gowans), 52 (Blickwinkel)

Corbis: 6 (Swim Ink 2. LLC), 10 (Hulton), 16 (Cinema Photo), 17 (John Springer Collection), 18 (John Springer Collection), 22 (J P Laffont/Sygma), 23 (Bettmann), 28 (EPA/Jason Szenes), 29, 31 (Bettmann), 45 (Francoise Demulder)

Dreamstime: 38 (Mike Brake), 41 (Pecak), 48 top (Sharon Agar), 53 (Jeff Dalton)

FLPA: 55 (Image Broker), 58 (Philip Perry)

Fotolia: 2 (Duncan Noakes), 34 (Andrey Kiealev), 37 (Samuel Rene Halifax), 39 (Tan Kian Khoon), 44 (Jim Knopf), 46 (Cynoclub), 50 (Junebreath), 51 (Jean-Marie Maillet)

Getty Images: 7 (Christian Science Monitor), 8 (Three Lions), 12 (Hulton), 24 (Frederick M. Brown), 30 (Vaughan Youtz), 43 (Viktor Drachev)

iStockphoto: 32 (Andreas Glossner), 35 (Richard Schmann), 59 (Marcel Pelletier)

Kobal Collection: 11, 27

Photos12: 19 (Archives du 7eme Art), 57 (Archives du 7eme Art)

Photoshot: 14 (UPPA), 20

Press Association: 40 (Melissa Phillip)

Rex Features: 13, 15 (PBS/Everett), 21 (NBCU Photobank), 26 (ITV), 35 (John Chapple), 48 bottom (Dan Callister), 54 (James Fortune)

TopFoto: 49 (Steve Warmowski/The Image Works)

ABOUT THE AUTHOR

Robert Grayson is an award-winning former daily newspaper reporter and magazine writer. He is the author of a number of books for young adults about environmental activism and law enforcement. His published work includes stories about working animals both on stage and in the movies. These have appeared in *Cat World*, *Animal Companion*, and numerous other animal-related publications. An avid cat lover, Robert's essays have appeared in the anthology *Pets Across America: Lessons Animals Teach Us*.